Kispiox River

Kispiox River

Arthur J. Lingren

Frank Amato
PORTLAND

River Journal

Volume 7, Number 3

Art Lingren has lived all his life in Vancouver, British Columbia, and after a 36 1/2-year career in regional government, he retired in January 2000. For most of his adult life, Art has traveled throughout British Columbia, as well as making the odd quest into neighbouring Alaska, Washington, Oregon and California, in pursuit of his favoured game fish, the steelhead. With a mound of experiences from these travels to call upon, and his passion for the history of the sport, he has authored *Fly Patterns of Roderick Haig-Brown*, *Thompson River Journal*, *Fly Patterns of British Columbia. Irresistible Waters, Dean River Steelhead Journal* and *Famous British Columbia Fly-Fishing Waters*.

Art first ventured to the Kispiox in 1974. During his many visits to the Skeena system since that first Kispiox visit, Art has spent the majority of his time fly fishing other Skeena tributaries. He became reacquainted with the Kispiox valley, river and people while researching material for *Famous British Columbia Fly-Fishing Waters*. Since that return to this fabled water, he makes sure that he puts aside a few days for the Kispiox River when he makes his trek north each year to fly-fish the Skeena system.

◆

Acknowledgments

Thanks to those who willingly lent a helping hand: Mark Beere, Jim Yardley, Bob Hooton, Bob Clay, Jim Adams, George McLeod, Wilfred Lee, Ginny Larson, Rick Miller, Loucas Raptis and Ray Makowichuk.

◆

About the Cover: *Kateri Clay setting up for a Spey cast.*

◆

Series Editors: Frank Amato
Kim Koch

Photography: Arthur J. Lingren (unless otherwise noted)
Fly plates photographed by: Jim Schollmeyer
Design: Kathy Johnson

Softbound ISBN: 1-57188-310-X; Hardbound ISBN: 1-57188-312-6
(Hardbound edition limited to 350-500 copies)

Frank Amato Publications, Inc.
P.O. Box 82112, Portland, Oregon 97282
www.amatobooks.com • 503.653.8108
Printed in Singapore
1 3 5 7 9 10 8 6 4 2

Kispiox River

KATHY JOHNSON

Kispiox River

◆

Introduction

Swoosh. I visualize it, I can hear it in my mind, and it gives me a surge of adrenaline when it happens, but. words cannot describe the rise of a summer-run steelhead to a surface-presented fly, especially the showy rises that happen when a bottom-dwelling summer-run all of sudden decides to quickly race to the surface and the water around your fly erupts like a volcano. On some rises the strike can be violent, while on others, the fly just disappears.

Bob Clay dropped me off upriver at 11 a.m., a late start for the long drift back to Bob's place on the Patch water, miles downstream. The most recent late-summer storm put the river out, but on this day the river had receded to the point where it was becoming low and clear. The overcast skies and occasional sprinkle, combined with the water conditions, made it ideal for fishing waked flies. I started at the head of a small piece of water, working and doing a two-step down to the tail. The size 8 Woolly Bear Bomber marked a clear wake as it chugged across the surface. Sometimes a half hitch on the

fly is needed to get the desired effect. But not this fly, yet. All of a sudden, the water's surface erupted near my fly, but the steelhead didn't take. I mused that if it was a running fish this might be its only rise. Travelers sometimes come violently at a waked fly, then rather than return to a lie, they carry on their upstream journey. But sometimes you just feel things are going to be okay. Today, I just felt good. It was going to be one of those days when you are just content to be alive and doing something you love. On those days things just happen.

A single Spey cast sent the fly out for its next drift and as the fly came over the lie the steelhead came again but missed. The fly chugged along a little more, the fish came again, missed again, and as the water shallowed, the surface erupted again, but the fish didn't get the fly in its mouth. Three times on one drift. I had an eager and active fish. Sometimes I will go down a size or two and, later in the day, on another fish going from a size-8 Bomber to a size-12 Skeena Bee did the trick. If a change of fly size doesn't work, I often will back

Under certain light and water conditions the steelhead will pounce on a waked fly.

up a few paces, change to a sparsely dressed black pattern and come through again. However, I was not ready to do any of those things yet. I wanted to work this pattern for a few more casts.

The single Spey cast shot the fly past the steelhead's lie. This time the steelhead was waiting. When the steelhead rose, the surface erupted and I felt the line go tight. About 15 minutes later I slipped the Woolly Bear Bomber from the jaw of the 33-inch, lovely-coloured, male, summer-run steelhead.

As the steelhead scooted back into the depths of the river I understood why fishermen from around the globe journey to Fay Davis's River of Dreams, the Kispiox.

The River and the Steelhead Season

The Kispiox River flows into the Skeena at Kispiox Village a few miles upstream from Hazelton. No other steelhead river in the world holds more allure to fly-fishers seeking large steelhead than does this stream. It is truly a river of dreams. Lured by the tales of its large steelhead, Fay Davis, a Californian, journeyed north to the Kispiox in 1973 where he became enamoured with this legendary river. Over his ten years of visits, Davis recorded his thoughts in a diary. Olga Walker persuaded Fay to publish his thoughts, and in 1984 he made a number of copies of his *River of Dreams* manuscript. This is what Davis had to say on the first day he saw the river in 1973:

> Here I stand: a dream come true. Excitement reigns so supreme that the hands are incoherent as I try lighting a cigarette. . . . Here I am, right on the banks of the mighty Kispiox. Never again can or will this initial compounded wedding of body and soul into an eternity-stopping, moment of dream realization come again. That moment is reserved for all of us in our one big dream come true, and right when we are most fully awake. Never will or can the memory of this exact moment be erased, and it will always be seen exactly as it was when time relented and hung still long enough for this to be recorded indelibly within my every fiber. And never again will the distinctive [comradeship] of my three friends, that shared in and perhaps watched my reactions to this live dream come true, be reenacted in just that way. . . I called it the Mighty Kispiox, and to me it will always be just that, even though it is not a big or mean river.

> On this particular day, September 6, it was low and clear, and probably could have been waded across at almost any point. . . . Yet, my inner vision portrayed where the steelhead must lie . . . . and as the years have come and gone since then, the steelhead have lain in the lairs of the brain's imaginary screen of the first encounter.

An angler fishes the water while the guide waits patiently in the raft.

The Kispiox River and Valley has smitten anglers for half a century and they come in droves during the late-August to mid-November steelhead season. Located well inside the coast mountain range, winter comes fairly early to this valley, and when temperatures plummet and ice takes hold along the river banks, usually the season is about done. The Kispiox closes on December 31. Most fly-fishers journey to this river for the September, October, and early November fishing. October is the big fish month.

Unless you are staying at one of the guide operations and they pick you up at the airport, you will need an automobile. Planes fly into Smithers and Terrace daily where rental cars are available. Eventually, whether you arrive by plane at Smithers or Terrace or you drive from your home wherever that may be, you will either be driving west from Smithers or east from Terrace to New Hazelton on Highway 16. At the west end of New Hazelton, turn off Highway 16 and take the old Hazelton turnoff and travel along it until you come to Kispiox Valley Road where you turn north (right). You will cross the Kispiox River bridge at Kispiox Village, after driving about seven miles on the Kispiox Valley Road. The Kispiox River has roads that parallel parts of the river, the main road for about 40 miles, along which you will find campsites,

Kispiox steelhead winter under the ice in the deeper pools.

lodges and resorts catering to fishermen. Reservations during peak season are advisable.

Early Sport Fishing

In 1866, the Kispiox Valley saw its first influx of white people. Telegraph workers arrived, running the line up the Kispiox Valley, but their work was of short duration and abandoned when another company completed a trans-continental telegraph link. Whether any of those workers tested the waters with rod and line we don't know. After the communications workers left in the early 1890s, missionaries settled in where the Sportsman Lodge is now. The first homesteaders arrived in the early 20th century, putting down family roots that remain to this day. In 1907, Wilfred Lee's great uncles were among the first settlers. Soon after, in 1910, Wilfred's grandfather homesteaded in the Sweetin River area. The valley's fish and game provided sustenance for the early white people just as it had for the First Nations people who have hunted and gathered in the valley since the earliest of time. However, sport fishing was not a part of First Nations or the lifestyle of the early settlers. As the Natives had done before

'SHOOT OUT'
In 1914 British Columbia's most famous 'shoot out' occurred here. Of the seven robbers who attempted to rob the Union Bank, three were shot dead by citizens, three were captured, and the seventh escaped with the money. In the previous year, robbers successfully removed from the same bank the then substantial sum of $17,000. intended for the railway builders payroll.

The Hazelton area has some interesting colourful stories, as this Highway 16 "Shoot Out" sign tells visitors.

them, the salmon, steelhead, trout and char were there for the taking, providing a valuable protein supplement through many months of the year, especially during the cold winter months. The river was their refrigerator and white settlers used the methods of the Natives to catch fish. A favoured Native method using roe was copied by the settlers. In the winter, the Natives would cut a hole in the ice-bound river and dangle a gob of salmon eggs to fish for wintering steelhead in the slow deep pools. To this day there are some favoured spots along the river where First Nations from Kispiox Village still harvest fish using this ancient method.

All the same, sport fishing was not the means for early white people in the Valley to catch their food. Early adventurers exploring Canadian Pacific Railway (CPR) routes through the Northern valleys, journeyed into the wilderness and tried their hand at fishing. In the 1880s, British adventurer J. Turner-Turner also made the journey up the Skeena, through Babine Lake then into the Fraser watershed and recorded his adventures in *Three Year's Hunting and Trapping in America and the Great North-West* (1888). Turner-Turner intended to winter at Kispiox, but the Natives fearing he was a land surveyor with the intention of taking away their land wouldn't allow it. He returned to the Forks and built a cabin on the point of land bordered by the Skeena and Bulkley rivers. This became his home until he continued his journey the following June.

During the September journey up the Skeena he noticed the salmon's abundance and tried spoon, Devon minnow and fly but could not entice them to take. Although he didn't catch any salmon, he did catch a fish he referred to as a sea-trout. He did not mention the size of the trout, and it could have been a cutthroat, bull trout or even small summer-run steelhead. It's unfortunate that he didn't winter at the Kispiox. Perhaps Turner-Turner might have caught some of the large Kispiox summer-run steelhead. However, he provides one of the earliest records of fly-fishing on the Skeena River, and records catching trout on the fly in the Babine River and Lake as well as from Stuart Lake and River on the Fraser watershed.

Dramatic events that took place in the first half of the 20th Century, such as World War I, the Depression and World War II, had adverse effects on travel into the North Country. The Kispiox Valley was quite remote and took considerable time and money for wealthy sportsmen to get to. Of course, fly-fishers were few in those days. After World War II and through the 1950s, roads were improved. With the completion of the new highway through the Fraser Canyon and local improvements to the highway through the Cariboo and west of Prince George to Prince Rupert, sportsmen found travel much easier and started venturing into the North Country in search of sport. In the early 1950s, steelhead catches from the

Anglers come from many places in the world to fly-fish for Kispiox steelhead. This group is an example: from L to R, Tom Bruns (leaning against doorjamb) is from Loveland, Colorado; Jim Adams, Berkley, California; John Bates, Billings, Montana; and Roger Still is from Edmonds, England.

The Seven Sisters peaks are a familiar sight to Skeena-system fly-fishers.

Skeena and Kispiox would bring worldwide attention to the area. In the October 1953 issue of *Northwest Sportsman* magazine, there is a picture of a man holding a large steelhead. The caption: "World Record Steelhead is this 30-lb. 8-oz. fish caught September 6th, 1953, by Jeff Wilson of Hazelton, B. C. at the mouth of the Kispiox River where it meets the Skeena. . . ." World-record fever brought many anglers to the banks of the Kispiox, but many came to fish other tributaries as well. The first record I have come across naming local and American steelhead fly-fishers and referring to a large steelhead from the Skeena system taken on the fly appeared on page 6 and 7 in the January, 1955 issue of *Northwest Sportsman*. In the article titled "Steelhead Grow Big," about his 1953 trip to the Skeena system and the Kispiox River, publisher Jim Railton writes:

> On our way north we met at Burns Lake a couple of keen steelheaders, Jeff Woodall and Cliff Cunnigham, who fish these steelies with a fly. In fact this Woodall chap ties all his own patterns and his pet river is the Morice . . . . Two days before I reached Hazelton, Jeff Wilson of Hazelton had caught a 30 1/2 pounder . . . .
>
> Naturally the publicity about such trophy fish by outdoor writers, press services of the transportation companies, attracted the attention of anglers interested to catch such fish. A party of anglers from Bakersfield, California visits this north-central area of B. C. every year. One of the party, Dr. Carl Moore, on his return home passing through Vancouver, called to say one of their party took a steelhead on the fly that weighed 28 pounds.

However, it was the catches shown below in the 1954 *Field & Stream* Trout, Western Division, Open Category contest that brought the Kispiox River to the notice of steelheaders throughout North America.

Chuck Ewart's first-place winner was also a new world record and with six of the top ten steelhead coming from the Kispiox that year, it became a destination fishery for those anglers seeking trophy-sized steelhead.

John Fennelly, an American from Lake Forrest, Illinois, fished the Kispiox for one day in 1954. He returned and spent eight days casting flies on the Kispiox during his month-long 1955 trip. About that river, the gear and fishing techniques as well as the anglers searching for that elusive record steelhead, he says:

> Unfortunately, the water was high and fairly muddy from heavy rains and crawling with spin fishermen from all parts of North America. Most of them has been attracted to the river by a story reporting two world record steelhead from the Kispiox in the fall of 1954, 36 and 33 pounds [note: this is an error. There was no 33-pound world record taken in 1954 in open-gear or fly-caught category]. In all, six of the ten largest steelhead recorded in 1954 had come from the Kispiox. . . . I landed just one steelhead of fifteen pounds and lost two others. . . . Although we did not see the fish, we were told that the Indians had netted a 41 pounder near their village at the mouth of the river.
>
> *Field & Stream* statistics for 1955 show an even more amazing record for the Kispiox. The six largest steelhead landed anywhere in 1955 on spinning tackle were taken from the Kispiox. These ran from 33 to 26 pounds. The three largest steelhead taken on flies also came from the Kispiox and ran from 29 to 26 pounds. Incidentally, my unreported 15 pounder was the same as the tenth largest fish taken on flies. (pp. 33-34)

Much of Fennelly's early Skeena system fly-fishing adventures, as well as later exploits, are recorded in his classic, *Steelhead Paradise* (1963).

1954 *Field & Stream* Trout, Western Division, Open Category					
Date	River	Weight	Lure	Angler	Placing
Oct. 5	Kispiox	36 lb.	T Spoon	Chuck Ewart	1
Oct. 24	Babine	31 lb. 14 oz	Spoon	Wendell Henderson	2
Oct. 1	Kispiox	31 lb. 8 oz.	Spoon	Arthur Mowett	3
Sept. 14	Kispiox	29 lb. 8 oz.	Spoon	Balthaser Goetz	4
July 1	Trout Lake	29 lb. 7 oz.	Plug	Joseph P. McDonnell	5
April 11	Kispiox	29 lb.	T Spoon	R. R. Keefe	6
Nov. 25	Kispiox	28 lb. 6 oz.	T Spoon	J. T. Schmidt	7
Nov. 30	Lake Pend Orielle	28 lb.	Plug	Orville Heath	8
Oct. 23	Kispiox	28 lb.	Spoon	Mrs. B. H. Woodruff	9
Jan. 6	Copper	27 lb. 12 oz.	Spoon	J. D. Williams	10

With Seven Sisters on the horizon, the Kispiox joins the Skeena River at Kispiox Village.

*George McLeod with his 29-pound 2-ounce, 1955 world-record,
fly-caught steelhead, later eclipsed by Mausser's 33-pounder.*

that at that time 70% of Kispiox anglers used lures and 30% used flies. The ratio of gear-to-fly anglers was probably higher in the years between 1950 and 1960. Fennelly observed in 1955 that fly-fishers were few, and the river crawled with spin-fishermen.

Those early fly-fishers persevered, searching the slower-moving runs with the fly. Some were rewarded with very large fish. Despite the fact that lure-fishers dominated the fishery, things changed over the next fifteen years. Many lurefishers left when *Field & Stream* discontinued its contests after 1977. Too many fishers were into catch and release and many of the trophy hunters stopped seeking that elusive world record, and by 1989, when catch and release became the rule on the Kispiox, most of the lure-fishers had left or switched to fly-fishing. At that time, creel statistics reported that the lure-fly gear ratio had been reversed. Now 80% of Kispiox anglers were using flies and 20% lures. Fly-fishing is now the method of choice by the majority of Kispiox anglers.

However, just as the spin-caught, world-record of 1954 brought the hordes of spin fishers, the *Field & Stream's* fly-fishing contest drew many fly-fishers to the Kispiox. This was especially so after George McLeod took a 29-pound, 2-ounce world-record steelhead on the fly in 1955, which was later eclipsed by Karl Mausser's 33-pound steelhead in 1962. Those large fly-caught monsters made this river a destination for many fly-fishers searching for big fish. It remains so to this day. On September 19, 1954, Bertram Woodruff took second prize in the *Field & Stream* Western Trout Fly-Casting category with a 19-pound, 8-ounce Kispiox steelhead. That was the first Kispiox *Field & Stream,* fly-caught, prize winner and of the 87 fly-caught, prize winners from British Columbia waters up to the contest's close in 1977, 60 came from the Kispiox River.

By the mid-1950s, fly-fishing for Kispiox steelhead had its disciples. They were not many, most, if not all, of those early fur-and-feather tossers were of American origin from Washington and California. The earliest Fisheries Branch creel survey done in 1974, that collected data on gear type, showed

The horses in the field across the river galloped around when I rowed the raft into this run.

Field & Stream Fishing Contest
Western Trout Fly-Casting Category
Kispiox Winners

Notes: 1. *Field & Stream* ran fishing contests for 67 years, starting in 1910.

2. In 1962, the Steelhead Trout Fly-Fishing Category was introduced. In 1966, after four years, the Steelhead Fly-Fishing Category was discontinued and entries reinstated in the Western Trout Fly-Casting Category. In addition, starting in 1962, *Field & Stream* published only the top three prize-winning fish.

Year	Date	Angler's Name	Weight	Placing	Fly Name
1954	September 19	Bertram H. Woodruff	19 lb. 8 oz.	second	Shrimp
1954	September 21	Louis Roux	15 lb. 8 oz.	sixth	Carson
1955	October 6	George W. McLeod	29 lb. 2 oz.	first (World Record)	Skykomish Sunrise
1955	September 24	Thomas E. Jacob	26 lb. 9 oz.	second	#4 Georgetta Coachman
1955	October 10	W. W. Thompson	25 lb. 10 oz.	third	Skykomish Sunrise
1955	September 17	Ralph Wahl	16 lb. 12 oz.	sixth	Yum-Yum
1955	September 16	Enos Bradner	15 lb. 12 oz.	eighth	Red Dragon
1956	September 19	Henry W. Perrott	23 lb. 15 oz.	first	Fall Favourite
1956	September 13	Donald V. Redfern	21 lb. 8 oz.	second	Marietta Special
1956	September 20	Dr. Charles B. Mincks	16 lb. 4 oz.	fifth	Red Hackle
1956	September 17	Al Knudson	15 lb. 4 oz.	eighth	Al's Special Spider
1957	September 21	Thomas E. Jacob	28 lb. 4 oz.	first	Skykomish Sunrise
1957	October 9	Ken McLeod	23 lb. 14 oz.	second	Skykomish Sunrise
1957	September 20	C. W. Johnson	22 lb. 12 oz.	third	Skykomish Sunrise
1957	October 7	George W. McLeod	21 lb. 9 oz.	fourth	McLeod Sunrise
1958	October 20	W. A. McMahon	14 lb.	third	Marietta
1959	October 6	Ken McLeod	22 lb. 8.5 oz.	first	McLeod Bucktail
1959	October 2	Kay Brodney	20 lb. 12 oz.	second	Fall Favourite
1959	October 13	John P. Walker	19 lb. 8 oz.	fourth	Skykomish Sunrise
1959	October 12	George W. McLeod	17 lb.	sixth	Skykomish Sunrise
1959	September 29	Donald V. Redfern	13 lb.	ninth	Marietta
1959	October 1	A. W. Hempleman	11 lb.	tenth	Marietta
1960	November 4	James R. Adams	20 lb. 4 oz.	first	Red Comet
1960	August 24	Otis Hart	20 lb.	second	Loon Fly
1960	October 20	Ken McLeod	17 lb. 3 oz.	third	McLeod Bucktail
1960	October 13	George W. McLeod	16 lb. 3 oz.	sixth	Skykomish Sunrise
1960	October 24	John P. Walker	16 lb. 13 oz.	fourth	Skykomish Sunrise

Year	Date	Angler's Name	Weight	Placing	Fly Name
1960	September 20	Donald V. Redfern	16 lb.	seventh	Marietta
1960	September 17	Robert M. Levison	15 lb. 4 oz.	eighth	Royal Coachman
1961	October 2	George McLeod	19 lb. 8 oz.	second	Skykomish Sunrise
1961	October 7	Ken McLeod	17 lb.	fourth	Skykomish Sunrise
1961	September 13	Adel Lockhart	14 lb. 8 oz.	ninth	Home-tied
1962	October 8	Karl Mausser	33 lb.	first (World Record)	Kispiox Special
1962	September 8	Forrest R. Powell	23 lb. 8 oz.	second	Royal Coachman
1962	October 13	John P. Walker	22 lb. 12 oz.	third	McLeod Ugly
1963	September 5	Cecil V. Ager	26 lb. 4 oz.	first	Home-tied
1963	October 14	Stephen E. Keough	26 lb.	second	Mausser Special
1963	September 20	Lawrence Lovelace	25 lb. 8 oz.	third	Skykomish Sunrise
1964	September 21	Alf. E. Sealey	23 lb. 2 oz.	first	Skykomish Sunrise
1964	October 17	Forrest R. Powell	21 lb. 4 oz.	second	Royal Coachman
1964	October 2	James R. Adams	18 lb.	third	Fire Orange
1965	October 12	Karl Mausser	25 lb. 1 oz.	first	Kispiox Special
1966	October 19	Andrew Jordan	30 lb. 2 oz.	first	Skykomish Sunrise
1966	September 25	Karl Mausser	27 lb. 2 oz.	second	Kispiox Special
1966	September 25	Kenneth B. Anderson	26 lb. 8 oz.	third	Skykomish Sunrise
1967	October 22	Forrest R. Powell	25 lb. 6 oz.	first	Sam 'n Daisy
1968	October 31	Forrest R. Powell	27 lb. 3 oz.	third	Royal Coachman
1968	November 8	John P. Walker	27 lb. 10 oz.	first	Thor
1969	October 28	Forrest R. Powell	26 lb. 10 oz.	first	Royal Coachman
1969	October 17	Troy J. Ceschi	23 lb. 12 oz.	third	Hand-tied
1970	October 24	Karl Mausser	27 lb. 8 oz.	first	McLeod Ugly
1970	September 21	Floyd L. Griesinger	27 lb. 8 oz.	second	Babine Special
1970	October 23	Ken McLeod	27 lb.	third	Gray Ugly Fly
1971	October 11	Donald D. Larson	27 lb.	first	Skykomish Sunrise
1972	September 25	Lawrence Lovelace	26 lb.	first	Skykomish Sunrise
1972	September 22	F. W. Brandenberger	22 lb.	third	Royal Coachman
1973	August 23	Willis C. Barnes	25 lb.	second	Home-made
1973	October 11	Donald D. Larson	24 lb. 10 oz.	third	Lorain
1974	November 1	Frederick H. Boyle	32 lb. 4 oz.	first	Home-tied
1974	September 15	Karl H. Mausser	26 lb.	second	Kispiox Special
1975	September 14	Floyd L. Griesinger	21 lb 4 oz.	first	Babine Fly

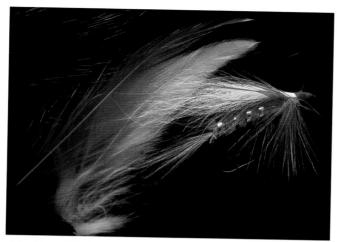

This Skykomish Sunrise dressed by George McLeod and developed by George and his father, accounted for 17 of the 60 Field & Stream, Western Trout Fly-Casting Category prize-winners.

Through the 1950s and early '60s, a number of American fly-fishers came to the Skeena and had lasting influences. Jack Horner, famous Californian fly tyer visited the Kispiox in 1954 and introduced flies such as the Horner Shrimp, Burlap, Thor, Polar Shrimp and Comet to the streams in the area. George and Ken McLeod from Washington state came in the mid to late 1950s, introducing to the Kispiox the Skykomish Sunrise, Purple Peril, McLeod Bucktail and McLeod Ugly. The McLeods took many *Field & Stream* prize-winning fish, topped by George's 29-pound, 2-ounce, world record, taken on a Skykomish Sunrise in 1955. At my request, George McLeod put together some of his recollections about his first trip, the river, its fish, and his world record. He writes:

My first trip to the Kispiox was in 1955 during the last week of September and the first week of October, with friends who had fished the lower river in early September 1954.

Four of us chartered a float plane to fly us from Smithers to Stephens Lake, near the headwaters of the Kispiox system. With two seven-man rubber rafts, we spent six days making the trip downstream to the Rodeo Grounds at the 17 mile bridge. We went through a lot of rough water and had to do a number of portages around very bad rapids and falls. On the second and third day, we fished about half the time and caught plenty of Dolly Varden to five pounds, 11 to 15 inch native cutthroat, some coho, but no steelhead. Heavy rains of the third and fourth days caused the river to rise and muddy, washing out the fishing. When we reached the big falls, coho and some steelhead were ascending the cascading rapids. With the river unfishable, we made long drifts over two days. With the worst water behind us, we reached

the Rodeo Grounds in the evening of the second day, the last hour of the drift in total darkness. It was a tough journey with little fishing, but we thoroughly enjoyed the experience. The large concentrations of eagles along the middle section of the river, feeding on salmon carcasses was quite remarkable. However, I do not recommend anyone drift the river above the large falls as the water is too dangerous, and the fishing is definitely much better in the lower river, once the run enters the system.

We made camp at the Rodeo Grounds and heard from friends that the fishing had been good earlier in the week before the river went out. The weather turned cold and on the next day, October 3, the water started to drop. By late afternoon there was two feet of visibility and I caught an 18 pounder below the camp. Bait fishermen also took

The once-abundant coho is making a startling comeback, thank to measures implemented by David Anderson when he was Minister of Fisheries.

*George McLeod with two steelhead, topping
20 pounds, taken in 1957.*

or 15 minutes. Two of the fish that were lost we thought were around 25 pounds apiece. What a great day it was for all!

Early on the morning of October 6th, the four of us drove up river to the Dundas farm and carried a seven-man raft across the field to the river bank. We had seen this piece of water a couple of days earlier but were on the wrong side to fly fish. After rowing across, we walked up the beach 175 yards and started fishing just below the very fast water. We spread out about 40 feet apart on this perfect piece of fly water, which was later became known a McLeod Riffle. Bill and Ollie started first with Webb and I to follow behind. Within five minutes Bill's reel was singing with a steelhead exploding across the surface of this wide run. He went down taking about 15 minutes to land and release the fish. In the meantime Webb tied into stubborn 20 pound male that would not leave the heavy current and it continued struggling

Fly-fishers probe both sides of the river on a misty fall morning.

four fish. On October 4th, we drove up river three or four miles to fish, but we found we were on the wrong side of the river to fly fish, with the exception of one hole. We hooked three, landing two before heading back to camp for lunch at 1 pm. At 3 pm Webb Thompson and I drove up to Wookey's place and parked at the edge of the road. We walked across a small field to the river and found a beautiful flat stretch of water. We stood on a low bank, admiring the drift in front of us, when a fish broke water in mid-stream. We rushed down the bank into the water and started fishing. On my fifth cast I hooked a fish, which I landed down the gravel bar near the tailout 20 minutes later. Webb lost one while I played mine. Every few minutes, a fish would break water along the 150 foot stretch in front of us. We had found a glory hole and continued to hook fish until dark. We hooked nine, landing six to 22 pounds.

On October 5th, four of us went down river and fisher the Upper and Lower Potato Patch holes. We hooked 10 fish by noon, landing six, releasing all. After lunch, we headed to Wookey's and the Glory Hole and found the run still holding a school of fresh-run, angry steelhead. We hooked 11 fish before dark, but only landed four. Some would jump a time or two and spit the hook while others would come unbuttoned after a fight of 10

upstream into the fast water. After considerable rod pressure, the fish finally took off downstream about 100 yards where it was landed and released.

It was a cold misty morning, but the four of us were ecstatic, fighting gorgeous, fresh-run steelhead. By 11 am we had hooked 12, landing eight, and all were released. After landing the 12th fish, I walked up the beach and watched my friends fish for 10 minutes or so. None of us had fished the really fast shallow water at the top of the riffle above where we had been hooking all the steelhead, so I decided to give it a try. I stripped out about 40 feet of line into the stripping basket and cast across the heavy current. The fly landed and was instantly engulfed in a tremendous swirl. The reel screamed as the huge male tail-walked downstream in front of my friends fishing below. We went up and down the beach, while the fish went all over the river trying to rid itself of the fly. For the first 30 minutes it didn't seem possible that I would land the fish, but finally it tired after 45 minutes and Webb was able to grab its tail and walk it out onto the gravel bar. Weighing in at 29 pounds 2 ounces, what a fish this thirteenth one of the morning turned out to be. With this whopping steelhead, we packed up and headed back to camp and left for Seattle that evening. In Seattle I had the fish mounted.

October 1955 was the start of our many-year love affair with the Kispiox River, its majestic scenery and the many friends we made in the valley and Hazelton. Through the late '50s, '60s and 70s we looked forward to our annual visits and the river's great fishing. It was a great pleasure for me to be able to share vacation time on this river with my dad, Ken McLeod, a devoted steelhead fly fisher. We had so many memorable experiences.

In 1957, Karl Mausser journeyed north from his California home and fished the Kispiox River for the first time. Mausser usually came north in May and fished for trout in the Babine. In August he set up camp on the Morice, then moved to the Kispiox in early October for the remainder of his stay. He will be remembered in the world of steelhead fly-fishing for his 33-pound, fly-caught world record. A fixture on the Morice, Bulkley and Kispiox for many decades, he named many of the pools. One Kispiox riffle favoured by Karl bears his name. On September 4, 2000, Mausser's family with many of the angling friends celebrated his life as a fly-fisher by depositing his ashes in the Morice River at By-Mac. In late 1988, I wrote Karl asking him for a picture of his world record. He was a trusting soul. If the roles were reversed, I am not sure if I would have lent my sole negative of that fish to a stranger.

Ken McLeod with a brace of 20-plus-pounders, taken in 1957.

About the picture of his world-record 33-pound steelhead and catch and release, Karl in a January, 1989 letter to me wrote that:

I'm enclosing my only negative of the fish so use and please return to me when you can. I'll be here in residence until April or May when I will start north. I usually cross the border around mid-May and head for the Upper Babine to enjoy some catch & release rainbow fishing. It's usually pretty good....

The [world-record] steelhead I caught in 1962 was 42 1/2" long and had a 24" girth—no one was with me at the time. It was formally weighed in [at] the back of Sergeant's store in Old Hazelton and was witnessed by Polly Sergeant and Drew Wookey. The fish weighed a bit more than 33 lbs. but, on a beef quarter balance scale the notches on the bar are at 8 oz. intervals or were at that time....

I wrote a factual account that night at Wookey's camp and a few years later a chap named Trey Combs was writing a steelhead book and contacted me and I let him use my story. It's there if you want it.

Part of the unpublished happenings are: I'd made the line myself based on a happening off Painter's resort some years before. And the fly which it took was something like a Skykomish and since I'd lost several to some sort of obstruction I felt when I tied it on having just lost another; that I didn't give a hoot if I lost it or not. Well the rest is history.

The fish was easy to capture. Maybe 10 minutes. One big problem; no gravel bar but it was so deep it [the fish] stranded on a mound of rubble close to the bank and I was able to jam my whole hand in the gill and out the mouth.

Of course these were the days with a 3 fish limit per day, nine in possession and catch and release wasn't even considered. We did release a lot but it wasn't a religion as it is today. I suggested to this [classified water and angling guide] task force that they consider making the Skeena drainage entirely catch and release, all species!!!

George McLeod was also on the river that day and writes:

For seven years my 29 pound 2 ounce steelhead was the world record, fly-caught steelhead until Karl Mausser caught his 33 pounder in 1962. The evening before Karl caught his big fish, he visited our camp at the Dundas farm. He had only eight pound leader and wanted to know what test leaders we were using. I gave him four leaders made from Bell, tapered 19, 16, 13. He did not tell us that for several days he had been seeing this big fish surfacing at the head of the shallow riffle leading into the Cottonwood Hole. On that particular trip, we fished the Cottonwood Hole almost every day for a couple of hours either in the morning or the afternoon. We never bothered with the shallow riffle 100 yards above the main part of the drift, a constant producer of fish.

If we were on the drift in the morning, Karl didn't fish it and he wasn't fishing in the afternoons while the world series were being broadcast. The day Karl caught his big fish, we too fished the Cottonwood. While we were fishing, Karl pulled his pickup on the shoulder of the road. Drew Wookey and he were returning from Hazelton where they had weighed a large fish on tested scales. Drew hollered that the fish weighed 33 pounds, a new world, fly-caught record and invited us to come for drinks at the camp on Karl. Mausser said that the fish didn't fight and headed right down to the small bar at the foot of the Cottonwood, taking only 10 minutes to land.

Through the 1960s, others came to see if they could latch onto a steelhead that would better Mausser's record. Others just came lured north by the prospect of adventure on distant and fabled waters. A youthful Jim Adams of Berkeley, California made his first trip in 1960. With four placing *Field & Stream* winners in the next few years, Jim, now a globe-trotting, fly-fisherman, antiquarian book and used collector tackle dealer, who is passionate about his sport, was a very forthcoming resource. Jim provided a number of interesting anecdotes about some of the early Kispiox regulars such as the McLeods, Mausser and Forrest Powell. When Adams and Mausser were taking 30 to 50 steelhead a month from the Kispiox, Powell was getting 150 to 175. His secret was to rush from pool to pool and rip a Scientific Angler "fisherman" or Wet Cel 1 through the water with a fast jerky retrieve. The big bucks in the Kispiox preferred a fly-fished deep and slow and Powell's technique, although productive, was selective for female steelhead.

Karl Mausser with his 33-pound world-record steelhead.

After World War II, as access became easier and sportsmen had more time, they came in dribbles at first to fish other Skeena River tributaries. Then attracted by reports in *Field & Stream* about world-record fish from the Kispiox, the river received international attention. When anglers first come into

Field&Stream
Fifty-Second
Annual Fishing Contest
Certificate of Award
FIRST PRIZE
this is to certify that
KARL MAUSSER   BURLINGAME, CALIF.
on the date inscribed below did hook and successfully land a
STEELHEAD TROUT
which has been weighed and measured, and a true record
thereof duly entered in the official register of the
Field & Stream Annual Fishing Contest

Date   OCTOBER 8, 1962
Weight   33 POUNDS
Length   3 FEET 6 1/2 INCHES
Class   FLY CASTING   Franklin S. Forsberg
                                                        Publisher
JUDGES: DR. C. W. GREENE   VAN CAMPEN HEILNER   A. J. McCLANE   DR. H. JOHN RAYNER

that they would survive for the late-spring spawning.

More often than not, the few anglers who practiced some form of catch and release in the 1950s through the 1970s did so because the steelhead was too small. Indeed, they were searching for big steelhead to kill and, if that big dead steelhead was a world record or *Field & Stream* contender, perhaps glory. Catch and release did not have the large following it has today. With such generous limits, sport fishers took their toll. Their harvest, when combined with the commercial catch that took on average 50% of the Skeena steelhead and a First Nations catch, led to a situation where there were simply too many people killing far too many fish. Something had to be done if this grand fish was to survive. Catch and release by sport fishers, a shorter season and less interception by the Natives and commercial fishermen have all had positive results on the Kispiox stocks of steelhead.

The Kispiox River has some fish arriving in late August, but the bulk of the run arrives later in September and October. Those seeking to capture a fabled Kispiox monster, plan their trip to coincide when the big fish migrate into the system, usually through October. Of all the Skeena watershed rivers, the Kispiox has a higher proportion of larger fish, with specimens in the 15- to 25-pound range quite common. And with some steelhead going into the 30-pound and larger range, this river provides the angler with chances at huge fish, but because of its accessibility and popularity, this river is often very crowded.

a lightly fished area, the resulting good catches attract others. The Kispiox and its tributaries became the destination for many sport fishers attracted by big fish and generous limits. From 1946 into the seventies, anglers could kill three steelhead a day and take home three-days' possession limit. In addition to the generous take-home limit, they could kill and eat fish during their stay. Through the 1970s into the late 1980s, daily limits were reduced from three to two, to one fish a day, and from three to two days' possession limit. In the 1970s, a yearly limit of 40 steelhead was imposed and this steadily declined through the 1980s until it was only one a year. In 1989 catch and release was imposed for the main-stem Skeena and tributaries above Cedarvale. The Kispiox has been a catch-and-release steelhead river since 1989.

In the early years, the sport fishing season was long. Most Skeena summer-run steelhead enter fresh water on their spawning migration through July, August and September. By early winter they have settled into holding pools, yet until the mid-eighties anglers continued to fish and kill them through the winter months, weather permitting. Note that one of the steelhead prize winners in *Field & Stream*'s 1954 contest was taken on April 11th. Winter is harsh in the upper Skeena watershed and the Kispiox Valley can be in a deep freeze from late October, but every now and then Chinook warming winds pass through or a mild winter permits fishing on some winter days. Regional Fisheries biologist and steelhead champion, Bob Hooton, closed the fishing on the Kispiox and all other Skeena tributaries above Cedarvale on December 31. He was determined that those fish surviving the commercial, Native and sport fisheries, would not be harassed as they matured and depleted stores of body fat into roe or milt and

The Kispiox's Summer-Run Steelhead

The world-famous Kispiox River steelhead enter the lower Skeena river a little later than early-run stocks destined for the Sustat and Morice systems. Migration for Kispiox fish usually begins around early August, peaking in mid to late August. With an average migration rate of around 3 to 4 miles per day, Kispiox fish appear to migrate slower through the Skeena than other upstream stocks. However, some fish do enter earlier and may travel quicker, because fly-fishers can find fish in the Kispiox around mid-August on any given year. The Kispiox River is nearly 100 miles long and perhaps these early arrivals are destined for the upper Kispiox and tributaries, such as the Sweetin and Nangeese rivers.

Steelhead stocks are specific to certain rivers, and stocks enter those rivers when water conditions provide ready access

The rain-swelled Sweetin River joins the Kispiox.

lived to spawn and pass on his genes to the wild fish native to the great Kispiox River.

Other Salmonids

The Kispiox River is home to the all species of Pacific salmons, steelhead, rainbows and cutthroat trout as well as bull trout (Dolly Varden). About the stocks of fish back in 1973, Fay Davis writes:

> That first year there were so many dead salmon on the banks that you could smell the river from two miles away. At Four-Mile you actually had to wade through spawned out carcasses to reach the water. Where ever you went there were hundreds of dog salmon jumping about, and if you happen to hook one you were wise to cut him loose because they are powerful, and will wear you out for no practical purpose. I already mentioned that coho were also everywhere we went. Another thing that first year, I have stood in one spot and caught from five to ten dollies, and cutthroat seemed to be everywhere. (*River of Dreams* p. 9)

In the early days of the Kispiox sport fishery there were good trout populations. However, too many anglers killing too many fish have depleted stocks and the bull trout (Dolly Varden) and trout are suffering. Nothing short of full catch-and-release for trout and char will reverse the harm done by too liberal catch limits over too many years. The July and August chinook fishery is attracting more and more fly-fishers each year with fish in the 40- to 50-pound range not uncommon.

In late August and September, coho start to show up and often take a fly. The coho were in serious trouble not that long ago. Just too high an exploitation from commercial, Native and sport fishers, and all user groups bear some responsibility for depleted coho stocks. However, the Kispiox as well as other Skeena system coho stocks are rebounding as a direct result of the Federal government's mid-1990s moratorium on killing coho by all users. However, it is the Kispiox's summer-run steelhead that attracts anglers from all over the globe.

Water Conditions

The Kispiox is a flashy river system affected by late-summer and fall rains. I remember my first trip to this river in 1974. We managed to catch a steelhead each on the day we arrived but that evening the rain started. The next morning the river was gone and we spent the majority of the week's holiday fishing the Skeena at Kitwanga, mostly for trout and Dolly Varden. Ideally you want the Kispiox to be on the fall and clearing to get the best fishing. In mid to late August the water temperatures will be in the low 50s during mid-afternoon. However, if it is a clear evening they can fluctuate about 5 degrees from early morning through to the afternoon. As the frosts of fall become more frequent, the river temperatures drop quickly on the Kispiox and through much of the season later in September and October you will find the water temperatures slipping down into the low 40s and into the high 30s if a cold spell lasts longer than a couple of days.

Winter does come early inside the Coast Range of mountains, and snow and icy banks are quite common throughout November. On a typical Kispiox Valley winter, the fishing will be finished some time in December. However, even in this cold country a warming wind, or Chinook as they are called, will allow some fishing to the locals until the December 31 closure.

Fly-fishing for chinook is becoming more popular not only on the Kispiox but other Skeena River tributaries as well.

Bright red rosehips decorate the banks.

fishing that morning with his wife Kathy, and with anchor ice along the banks, Bob caught an 8-pounder that rose to a waked dry fly. Kathy using the traditional sunk-line technique beached three. Even in the most trying conditions, you never know what will happen. However, because of the nature of the river, its fish and the fact that steelhead are bottom-dwellers, the sunk-line is the staple technique on the Kispiox.

When observed in their river environment, most salmonids will be seen close to the bottom. The observation of this phenomenon hundreds of years ago prompted anglers to fish down to them. The Kispiox River steelhead are no different from other salmonids; they lie close to the bottom.

The equipment for this type of fishing varies and the fly-fisher needs to come equipped with lines and flies that marry to water conditions, especially after a spate when the river is dropping and clearing. In murky but clearing water, you can't catch a steelhead if the fish can't see your fly. Large flies, three inches or longer, are the order of the day for sunk-line fishing.

Many steelheaders rely solely on the sunk-line method for catching steelhead on the Kispiox; it is certainly the most productive technique. But sometimes opportunities knock and when they do a fly-fisher should be adaptable and take advantage of the situation. Enticing a steelhead to a surface-presented fly is one of the thrills of the sport.

Using a floating line and fishing a wet fly just under the surface, or a dry fly in tension and waked across the surface can be effective if used when the water and light conditions suit these techniques. In 1987, Ed Exum took one steelhead on a waked dry fly that was 44 1/2 inches long with a 23 1/2-inch girth. According to the Sturdy table that fish was close to Mausser's world-record, fly-caught 33-pounder. The Princess of Italy, one of Wilfred Lee's guests, not too long ago landed one fish that was around the 25-pound-plus range on a waked dry fly.

When steelhead settle into holding pools some anglers will fish an upstream deeplysunk wet fly to the bottom-dwellers.

Indeed, opportunities exist on the Kispiox to experiment with different fly-fishing techniques. However, combining the right fly pattern with presentation and water and light conditions is critical for consistency, not only on the Kispiox, but on all steelhead rivers.

Tackle: Come Prepared

Before we get into fly patterns, a word about tackle is appropriate. The Kispiox is a fairly large steelhead river with strong and some exceptionally large fish. Eight, nine and even number 10 fly-fishing outfits are the order of the day, whether using single-handed or double-handed rods. You should have a floating line and be able to use interchangeable sinktips in a variety of densities and lengths from 10 to 24 feet. Single-handed rod users should have besides a floating line, lines

Methods of presentation

There are five basic methods of presenting flies to steelhead: floating-line, skated- or waked-fly, sunk-line, dry-fly, and upstream sunk-fly presentations. The Kispiox River offers opportunities for four of the five techniques. During late summer and fall into winter, fly-fishers visiting the Kispiox will be fishing a declining water temperature regime, with periodic increases due to weather fluctuations. The colder the water, the less inclined steelhead are to rise to the surface to take flies. However, they can be caught on a waked fly in some pretty cold water on this river. I talked with Bob Clay after Christmas as I was working on this manuscript. He had been

Purple asters add colour to the river's gravel bars.

Some steelhead fly-fishing tools.

that are equal to the Teeny 200 and 300 for sunk-line fishing.

Anglers should come to the Kispiox with a spare everything from rod, reel, sinking and floating lines, waders, to boxes of flies. Bob Clay does sell some fishing supplies such as rods, lines, sink tips and flies, but if other gear is needed then it is at least a couple or more hours drive away to Smithers' or Terrace's flyfishing shops. The weather in the early part of the season can be pleasant, but as fall progresses it will get cold. Neoprene waders or at least neoprene-booted breathable waders with fleece clothing are a must. Felt-soled wading boots will do the trick over studded boots. A good rain coat to keep you dry is a must, and gloves without fingertips help somewhat to keep the hand from numbing on those cold frost-filled days. Come prepared for wet and cold weather.

Fly Patterns

The Kispiox is unique in that it has large fish but it is an understatement to say that it can be affected by fall rains. The river can rise rapidly and become terribly muddy and be out for days. When the rains stop and the river starts to clear and recede, that is the time you want to be there. Steelhead fly-fishers need to consider all the following factors when choosing their fur-and-feather enticements.

- Height of river and muddy water conditions: to what depth can you see river bottom.
- Other water conditions: temperature, velocity, and surface turbulence.
- Light conditions: whether it is sunny, cloudy or the water is shaded.
- Time of the day: early morning, mid-day, evening.
- State of the fish: fresh-run or present in the river for some time.
- Method of presentation.

When fishing conditions deteriorate, the skillful, knowledgeable and adaptable fly-fisher shines over those average-skilled ones. By marrying fly-fishing method to conditions and fly selection, a competent fly-fisherman can often catch fish even under the most trying conditions. Also, on a long river such as the Kispiox that rises and falls quickly, and with 40 miles of upriver access road, the angler should keep in mind that the upper stretches will clear and become fishable a day or two sooner than the lower reaches.

To avoid wasting time trying different types of flies, concentrate more on matching technique with conditions and keep fly choices to a minimum.

There are diver patterns from which to choose—just look at any steelhead fly-fishing book; the selection is almost limitless. The following list includes some old, tried and tested, as well as current local favourites.

Keep in mind, however, that fly patterns are legion and there are no absolute rules for their use and other patterns similar in shape, size and colour will work just as well as the local favourites.

Old Favourites

The patterns of the 1950s and 1960s that came to the Kispiox with Washington and California fly-fishers have fallen from disfavour over the years. However, for posterity they deserve a place in this book. Perhaps, too, some keen anglers will dress and swim the old favourites through the lies that George McLeod and Karl Mausser took their world-record fly-caught steelhead.

Skykomish Sunrise

Tag: Flat, silver tinsel.
Tail: Red and yellow hackle sprigs mixed.
Body: Red chenille.
Throat: Red and yellow hackle.
Wing: White bucktail.

Black and Blue Tube Fly

Slime Sucking Leech

Green Thing

Egg Sucking Leech

Stellars Jay

Green Slimer

Popsicle

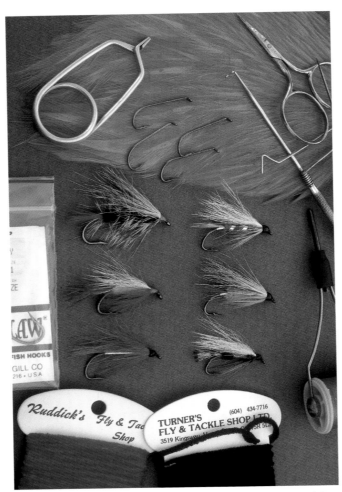

These six old Kispiox patterns accounted for nearly two thirds of the 60 Field & Stream, Western Trout Fly-Casting *prize winners.*

Royal Coachman Bucktail

Tail: A few sprigs from a golden pheasant tippet feather.
Body: Peacock herl, scarlet floss and peacock herl.
Throat: Brown hackle.
Wing: White bucktail.

The Royal Coachman was the most well-known wet fly during the 20th Century. The bucktail version has a long history on western waters waters and even this famous fly has fallen from disuse and is rarely seen in the fly boxes of today's steelheaders. However, topped with Forrest Powell's 1968 third-place prize winner of 27 pounds 3 ounces and Powell's 1969 first-place prize winner of 26 pounds 10 ounces, and with a total of six *Field & Stream* Kispiox prize winners to its credit, this fly comes in a distant second when compared to the Skykomish Sunrise.

McLeod Ugly

Tail: Fluffy red hackle fibres.
Body: Black chenille.
Hackle: Grizzly wound along body.
Wing: Black or plain bucktail.

This was one of the first large black-bodied flies used for steelhead on the Kispiox River and is another fly coming from George McLeod's vise. Combs, in his book *Steelhead Fly Fishing & Flies* (1976), claims that McLeod developed this pattern in 1962. In 1959, however, Ken took first place in the *Field & Stream* contest with a 22-pound 8 1/2-ounce Kispiox steelhead taken on a McLeod Bucktail and George McLeod provided pictures of steelhead taken on a McCleod Ugly on the Kispiox River as early as 1957. One thing is certain, the McLeod Ugly was a staple pattern on this river since the late 1950s. Karl Mausser was fishing a McLeod Ugly when he took the 1970 *Field & Stream* first-place winner of 27 pounds, 8 ounces from the Kispiox.

Kispiox Special

Tail: Red polar bear fur.
Body: Hot orange wool or chenille.
Throat: Red hackle.
Wing: White bucktail.

As I prepared to write this journal, Mausser's good friend and Morice River guide Ray Makowichuk sent me some photographs of Mausser's 33-pound world-record fly-caught Kispiox River steelhead. Ray obtained the photos from Rick Miller, Mausser's grandson. The mounted world record includes the fly that Karl used on that historic day back in 1962. Most books that give a dressing for the Kispiox Special tell you to use a body of hot orange chenille, however, the actual fly that the monster steelhead took was dressed with hot orange yarn and not chenille. Mausser's Kispiox Special accounted for five *Field & Stream* Kispiox prize winners.

This famous steelhead pattern was originated for the Skykomish River by Washington State, father/son steelhead fly-fishing team Ken and George McLeod. In use for a number of years, it became well-known out of the state in 1954 when W. W. Thompson took a 20-pound 8-ounce steelhead from waters around Hazelton. The information provided by Thompson did not say whether he caught the steelhead in the Skeena or Bulkley, which joins the Skeena at Hazelton but that Skykomish Sunrise-caught steelhead took first prize in the 1954 *Field & Stream*, Western Division, Trout Fly-Casting Category. Next year in 1955, George McLeod journeyed north and landed a whopping fish of 29 pounds 2 ounces, a new world-record and first-prize winner in the *Field & Stream* contest. That fish took a Skykomish Sunrise. From 1955 through to 1977, the Kispiox River accounted for 60 prize-winning *Field & Stream* fly-caught trout (steelhead), 17 were taken on the Skykomish Sunrise. No other fly used on that river during those years can come close to the Skykomish Sunrise's record.

Flash Bug

Moose Hair
Lambroughton Skater

Pink-Purple
Bomber

Sofa Pillow

Kispiox Caddis,
Tan

Kispiox Caddis,
Black

Horner Silver Shrimp

Horner Orange Shrimp

Moose Hair
Totem Stone

McLeod Ugly

Thor

Kispiox Special

Royal Coachman
Bucktail

Sykomish Sunrise

Marrietta

Red comet

Fall Favourite

Amazingly, not one is less than 25 pounds and, of course, the list is topped by Karl's 33-pound, fly-caught world record.

Marrietta

Tag: Flat, silver tinsel
Tail: A few sprigs of red hackle.
Body: Fluorescent flame chenille.
Throat: Fluorescent orange hackle.
Wing: Natural bucktail.

Donald Redfern invented this pattern back in the 1950s and used it frequently on his trips north to the Kispiox River. With five *Field & Stream* fly-caught prize winners, three taken by Redfern, it became a standard Kispiox pattern.

Fall Favourite

Tail: None.
Body: Flat, silver tinsel.
Throat: Red hackle.
Wing: Orange bucktail or polar bear.

California fly-fishers brought this popular Golden Gate State favourite to the Kispiox River in the mid-1950s. With the Fall Favourite on the end of their lines, Henry Perrott took first prize in the *Field & Steam* 1956 contest with a 23-pound, 15-ounce Kispiox steelhead, and Kay Brodney took second prize in the 1959 contest with a 20-pound, 12-ounce Kispiox steelhead.

Red Comet

Tail: Red polar bear or substitute bucktail as long as hook shank.
Body: Oval, silver tinsel.
Throat: Red and white hackle.
Wing: None
Head: Silver bead chain.

This is another favourite from California that was introduced to the Kispiox River during Jack Horner's visit in the mid-1950s. Using a Red Comet, Jim Adams from Berkeley, California took first place in the 1960 *Field & Stream* contest with a 20-pound 4-ounce Kispiox steelhead.

Thor

Tail: Orange hackle sprigs.
Body: Red chenille.
Throat: Brown hackle.
Wing: White bucktail.

The Thor was developed in 1936 and named by Jim Pray for local California fly-fisher Walter Thornson after he took the 1936 *Field & Stream* contest's first place with an 18-pound Eel River steelhead on this new pattern. It soon became a Northwest favourite and made its way north to the Kispiox with California fly-fishers. With a 27-pound 10-ounce Kispiox steelhead on a Thor, John P. Walker took first prize in the 1968 *Field & Stream* contest.

Horner Silver Shrimp

Tail: Deer hair.
Body: Flat, silver tinsel.
Hackle: Grizzly wound up body.
Back: Bucktail pulled over back and lacquer.
Head: Black with painted eyes.

Another California fly of 1930's vintage that found its way north in the 1950s. Jack Horner, well-known San Francisco fly tyer introduced this pattern and his Orange Shrimp to the Skeena system in 1954. The Orange Shrimp is similar to the Silver, however, there is no body hackle and the orange shrimp has an orange hackle throat. *Field & Stream* records show only one Kispiox prize-winning steelhead taken on a shrimp pattern. It is Bertram Woodruff's 1954 second place, 19-pound, 8-ounce prize winner.

Contemporary Kispiox Patterns

All those early patterns were used on a sinking line and fished down to the steelhead. Many of the contemporary patterns were designed for that technique—it is the more productive flyfishing technique. Nonetheless, many fly-fishers like to bring steelhead to the surface to take a fly. Anyone who has experienced it will tell you that a surface explosion from a steelhead chasing a waked fly is one of the great thrills of steelhead fly-fishing. Many of the following patterns come from Bob Clay's fly box and are of his own adaptations. Bob and I talked about fly development and we both agree that nothing is really new, rather we take ideas from others and combine our own idea that suits our angling philosophy and transfer that into a fly. As a result we often alter an old pattern by changing a colour or adding some new fly-tying material and attach a new name. Fly development is in continual evolution. Steelhead do respond to certain things in a fly. For example, moving parts attract fish, incorporating feathers and materials that fluctuate, flutter and gleam as they are brought across the current does entice steelhead.

The following patterns for the sunk- and waked-fly techniques come from the fly boxes of Kispiox fly-fishers such as Bob Clay, Jed Clay, Wilfred Lee, Wally Bolger, Dick Dirkson, and Don Williams. They are today's popular steelhead patterns and are just what the doctor ordered to catch the Kispiox's mighty and elusive monsters of the deep.

Popsicle

(Contributed by Jed Clay)
Hook: Eagle Claw 182, size 1.
Tail: None.
Body: Orange and red marabou with a few strands of orange and pearlescent flashabou.
Collar: Purple marabou.
Head: 5/32 Groovy eyes.

A cow moose with calf nibbling on the river's-edge foilage.

This version of the Popsicle is dressed on a long-shanked hook with an attachment line of 30-pound Fireline for the Eagle Claw trailing hook.

Egg Sucking Leech

(Adapted and contributed by Bob Clay)

Hook: Eagle River 1/0 salmon.
Thread: Neon flat waxed nylon.
Body: Neon flat waxed nylon.
Hackle: Black marabou with a few strands of pink Krystal Flash.
Head: Pink chenille.

Slime Sucking Leech

(Adapted and contributed by Bob Clay)

Hook: Eagle River 1/0 salmon.
Thread: Lime green flat waxed nylon.
Body: Lime green flat waxed nylon.
Hackle: Black marabou with a few strands of lime green Krystal Flash.
Head: Lime green chenille.

Stellars Jay

(Originated and contributed by Wally Bolger)

Hook: Gamakatsu Octopus Blue No. 4.
Thread: Black flat waxed nylon.
Body: Blue tinsel.
Hackle: Light blue followed by dark blue marabou with a few strands of blue Flashabou and Krystal Flash.
Collar: Black marabou.
Head: 5/32 Groovy eyes.

This pattern is dressed on a long-shanked hook with an attachment line of 30-pound Fireline for the Gamakatsu trailing hook.

Green Slimmer

(Originated and contributed by Wilfred Lee)

Hook: Eagle River 1/0 salmon.
Thread: Lime green flat waxed nylon.
Body: Lime green flat tinsel.
Hackle: Lime green marabou with a few strands of lime green Krystal Flash and Flashabou.
Head: Lime green chenille.

Green Thing

(Originated by Dirk Dirkson and contributed by Bob Clay)

Hook: Eagle Claw 182, size 1.
Thread: Green flat waxed nylon.
Tail: Black marabou with a few strands of green Flashabou and Krystal Flash.
Body: Green cactus chenille.
Hackle: Natural black Jersey giant.
Head: Brass cone head.

This pattern is dressed on a long-shanked hook with an attachment line of 30-pound Fireline for the Eagle Claw trailing hook.

Black & Blue tube fly

(Originated and contributed by Bob Clay)

Tube: Plastic.
Thread: Black flat waxed nylon.
Tag: Blue tinsel.
Tail: Black marabou with a few strands of blue Flashabou and blue Krystal Flash.
Body: Blue tinsel.
Wing: Collar of black marabou with a few strands of blue Flashabou and blue Krystal Flash.
Head: 5/32 brass groovy eyes.

Kispiox Caddis, Tan
(Originated and contributed by Bob Clay)

Hook: Tiemco 105, size 6.
Tail: Orange Flashabou.
Body: Orange Phentex.
Hackle: Grizzly
Wing: Natural whitetail deer.

Kispiox Caddis, Black
(Originated and contributed by Bob Clay)

Hook: Tiemco 105 size 6.
Tail: Blue Flashabou.
Body: Black Phentex.
Hackle: Grizzly
Wing: Black-dyed whitetail deer.

Pink-Purple Bomber
(Originated and contributed by Bob Clay)

Hook: Tiemco 105, size 4.
Thread: Neon, flat, waxed nylon.
Tail and Wing: Pink-purple moose-hair tips.
Body: Flared and clipped, pink-purple moose butt hair.

Moose Hair Lambroughton Skater
(Originated by Dave Lambroughton and
contributed by Don Williams)

Hook: Tiemco 105

Tail, Back and Wing: Black moose hair.
Thread and Body: Red, flat, waxed nylon.

Moose Hair Totem Stone
(Contributed by Don Williams)

Hook: Tiemco 9375, size 4.
Thread: Brown, 6/0 UNI-thread.
Tail: Two, dark brown, goose quill segments.
Body: Olive brown, polar bear or synthetic dubbing.
Rib: Medium oval, gold tinsel.
Hackle: Red game cock.
Wing Case: Moose body hair.

Sofa Pillow, Stimulator
(Contributed by Don Williams)

Hook: Tiemco 200R
Thread: Fluorescent red.
Tail: Elk hair.
Body: Mix of dyed orange polar bear and synthetic seal fur.
  (U.S. tyers use synthetic seal fur only.,
Rib: Small, oval gold tinsel.
Body and Head Hackle: Red game cock.
Wing: Elk hair.

Flash Bug
(Contributed by Don Williams)

Hook: Tiemco 3761, size 6 or 4.
Thread: Black or brown 6/0.

Bears are common in the valley.

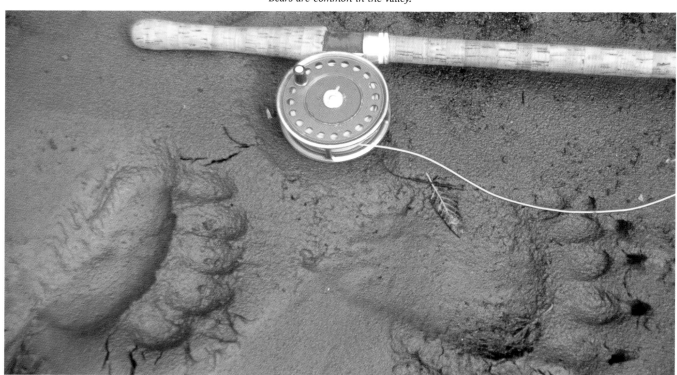

A sow with a couple of cubs.

Tail: Chartreuse Krystal Flash.
Butt: Peacock herl.
Body: Spun and clipped, natural deer hair.
Hackle: Red game cock.

Kispiox River Regulations

The Kispiox River is in Management Region 6 and is closed to all angling from January 1 to June 15. Anglers wishing to fish for steelhead must purchase a steelhead tag. Specific regulations that apply to the Kispiox are: bait-ban, non-retention of steelhead, no angling from boats, no power boats, and it is a classified water from September 1 to October 31. During the classified water period, non-British Columbia Canadians and non-residents of Canada must pay a day fee to fish the Kispiox. On their Classified Waters, licensed, non-BC anglers must enter the date prior to commencing fishing in the morning, and angling licenses must be carried on person while on the river. British Columbia residents must have an annual Classified Waters license to fish this river, which allows BC resident anglers access to all British Columbia's classified waters. Additional information on Region 6 waters is found in the *BC Fresh Water Fishing Synopsis.*

The classified waters management system has had its problems since it was implemented in the early 1990s. For about five years, government has attempted to do something to improve the classified waters and angling guide management system. However, for a number of reasons the review has faltered, stopped and sputtered to life again and again. As I write this in the winter of 2003, the government has brought together a group of stakeholders from the angling public and the guiding industry to provide input into the Angling Guide Management and Classified Waters Review. On January 16, 2003, I attended the preliminary resident anglers' meeting to discuss our concerns. After that meeting

concluded, the delegates from organized and independent anglers joined guide industry representatives and government staff for a two-day Angling Guide Management and Classified Waters Review workshop. This group did reach a consensus opinion on how to change and better manage British Columbia's special waters. The review needs to play out in the coming months, but in all probability the Kispiox River and its over-subscribed fishery will be affected by this review.

The Kispiox River Wilderness Experience

The Kispiox Valley has been inhabited by First Nations people for 3000 years, white people have settled and farmed and ranched in the valley for 100 years. The Kispiox wilderness experience is not like an uninhabited river such as the Dean River, but on any given day, while floating the river or driving along the valley roads, you will see wildlife. Bear, moose, deer, eagles and all other kinds of feathered and furry creatures inhabit the forest along the river's edge or the banks of the river. An endangered species not that long ago, whooping cranes making their journey to southern parts stop and feed in some of the farmers' fields. And occasionally, as you cast your fly in the late summer and early fall, you will hear their peculiar whooping call on their migration to distant lands.

Fly-fishers tossing their feathered creations to Kispiox steelhead will find a valley filled with friendly folk, some who will let you trespass through their land to fish the river. However, courtesy dictates that you ask before you trespass. A map showing some of the names of fishing holes is included in this treatise. Most of the named holes are in the lower 20 miles of river, but the water further up does have some water that will hold fish. Steelhead do migrate though the Lower Kispiox to spawn in the Sweetin, Nangeese and Upper Kispiox. However, the further up you go, the fewer fish you will find. Also, Kispiox steelhead hold in the Skeena River,

The figures that are carved provide the outline for the story that goes with the pole.

Services in the Valley

Liquor and Groceries: The Kispiox Valley is about 1/2-hour drive from Hazelton, located at the junction of the Bulkley and Skeena River. Hazelton offers full visitor services. For those fishermen who like to cap the day off with a wee dram of whisky or other spirit, the liquor can be obtained at the Hazelton liquor store. Hazelton also has the closest grocery store.

First Nations Services: Gitxsan First Nations people have lived at near the mouth of the Kispiox River since time immemorial. The Native people are an influential force in the valley and much of the Lower Kispiox River from the Patch Water to the mouth flows through Gitxsan land. Fishing and camping permits that allow a fisherman to access that section of river flowing through Native land, can be obtained at the Band Council office in the village. There is a gas station and convenience store in Kispiox Village.

First Nation's Crafts: For those wanting to go home with a reminder of the area, Gitxsan crafts are available at the Kispiox Cultural Centre, located just over the Kispiox River bridge and on the left-hand side kitty corner to the gas station. Phone: 250.842.7057, email: info@kispioxadventures.com

My wife doesn't go on these fly-fishing adventures with me and after well over 30 years of marriage I need new ideas for birthday and Christmas gifts. First Nation's carved jewelry makes a good birthday or Christmas present. The silver trout-head pendant featured with the McLeod Ugly fly was carved by a Gitxsan artist and it saved me from doing last-minute Christmas shopping in 2002.

First Nation's Eco-Expeditions: For those fishermen wanting a break from fishing or just wanting to learn a little more

upstream and down of the Kispiox mouth and although it is big water to fish, it can be productive.

A spate river, the Kispiox runs are subject to change with each flood event. Some runs will be good one year and not so good the following, while some runs remain stable for years or even decades. I will not tell you which runs are the better more productive ones, fly-fishing for steelhead is an adventure and discovery is part of any adventure.

Drifting in a raft is a popular way to fish the Kispiox. A public road runs upriver past the Nangeese River and by exploring a little you will find places to put-in. Fly-fishers are a talkative group and are often willing to share knowledge and tips on access and where to fish. Those tips may be gleamed from other fly-fishers that you meet in the resorts, campsites, the restaurant or on the river. However, no fisherman wants too much competition so don't expect to get the total unabridged Kispiox River secrets without some effort.

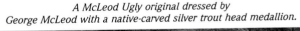

A McLeod Ugly original dressed by George McLeod with a native-carved silver trout head medallion.

At Riverwatch Fly Rods, master craftsman, fly tyer and guide Bob Clay, builds bamboo and graphite fly rods and keeps a small stock of fly-fishing supplies.

about the area, Skeena Eco-Expeditions Gitxsan guides will take you on river rafting and hiking tours on which you can explore their traditional territory and observe their culture. Phone: 250.842.7057, Toll free: 1.877.842.5911, or email: info@kispioxadventures.com

Kispiox Valley Fishermen's Services

Riverwatch Fly Rods: Bob Clay came to Kispiox Valley in the '70s, loved the valley and its fish and stayed eventually building a beautiful house overlooking the river. A guide on the river for years, he knows the river intimately.

Over the years when I saw Clay at Steelhead Society meetings or as he drifted with John Baigent and visited the Totems camp on the Dean River, Bob has extended numerous invitations to come fish the Kispiox. Years had lapsed since I had thrown a line in this famous river and I eagerly

Bob Clay searching the run below his home using one of his hand-crafted bamboo double-handed fly rods.

approached the top of the run. Spey casting about 70 to 80 feet of line, I sent the No. 2 Black General Practitioner on the end of my sink-tip over the water and worked my way a pace or two at a time down the run. A fishy pool from which the Clay family had hooked half a dozen fish earlier, I was not surprised when my line stopped in mid-drift and I felt something solid when I stuck. Sometimes steelhead are slow to react, but from experience I knew it was a fish and not bottom. After an exciting struggle, I slid a 31-inch female into shallow water. I had fished only 10 minutes. Bob joined me a little later and

Lead by the head Tom Turkey, a whole flock of turkeys escorted me to the riverbank.

took a fish around 32 inches on his new experimental Clay-built double-handed bamboo rod.

Farm chores took Bob away from the river and I was left to myself again. The Kispiox was good to me that afternoon with six steelhead hooked and three landed. Sometimes luck plays a part when fishing. I had come from the Bulkley that morning more to see the river and Bob, but experienced excellent sport.

Clay sold his guide days to Wilfred Lee a few years ago and now guides for Wilfred during the steelhead season. Bob is a man of many talents, one of them is his skill at turning Tonkin grass into bamboo rods. Clay builds double- and single-handed bamboo fly rods, custom orders only. As well, he usually has a few double- and single-handed graphite fly rods for sale and does rod repairs. Other fly tackle available at his rod-building shop includes custom-tied, local-favourite fly patterns dressed by Bob or his daughter Kali, and he does have a small stock of fly lines and sinking-tips. Clay's Riverwatch Fly Rod sign is located on the river side of the road about four miles from Kispiox Village near the end of the graveled portion of the Kispiox River Road. Phone: 250.842.6447, email: riverwatchrods@yahoo.ca

Sportsman Kispiox Lodge: Located on the forest side of the road just a short distance below the Rodeo Grounds, the Sportsman Kispiox Lodge is a focal point in the valley for fishermen. Built by Gary Wookey in 1965 and sold shortly after to Patrick and Margaret Clay (no connection to Bob Clay). Margaret Clay operated the lodge after her husband passed away, selling it to Allan and Ginny Larson in the late 1990s. It was in behind the lodge that the first missionaries into the valley settled in the 1890s. The missionaries made and sold clay bricks to support their existence. Meals, accommodation, guide service, fishing licenses, flies and some local crafts are available at the lodge. It is the only restaurant in the valley and is licensed to sell liquor with meals. Phone: 250.842.6455, email: allanlarson@uniserve.com

Kispiox Steelhead Resort, Olga Walker's former camp, is located on Popular Park Road.

Kispiox Steelhead Camp: For years Olga Walker was the steelheading grand dame in the Kispiox Valley. Her camp, which offers housekeeping units and sells fishing licenses to guests, is located on the river's right bank across the road and not far from the spot where Karl Mausser took his world-record, fly-caught steelhead in 1962. Now in her 80s, she has retired and moved to Smithers to spend her golden years. When she retired, Olga sold the camp to Helmut and Andrea Krenn. Phone 250.842.5435 or 250.847.6007.

Ginny Larson and husband Allan own the Sportsman Kispiox Lodge, a gathering spot for visiting fly-fishers.

Kispiox River Resort and Campground: Located on the right bank of the river along Poplar Park Road, built by Drew Wookey back in the 1950s, the Kispiox River Resort and Campground was the first steelheading camp on the Kispiox River. This is where Karl Mausser, Ken and George McLeod, Enos Bradner, Al Knudson, Forrest Powell and countless other early-day fly-fishers called home while on their Kispiox adventure. Jim Sayles is the current proprietor. Rustic cabins of a long-ago vintage provide the angler with a warm dry place to rest weary bones after a long day on the river. Other services offered at Sayles' resort include full-service hook-ups for recreation vehicles, tent sites, hot showers, flush toilets, laundry,

River's Edge Campground is located on the lower river.

Kispiox River Resort and Campground was the valley's first resort catering to fishermen.

and a 9-hole pitch and putt golf course. Fishing licenses are available as well. Phone: 250.842.6182 or off season 928.565.2615.

River's Edge RV and Camping: Located on the left bank of the Kispiox River a short distance downstream of the Sportsman Kispiox Lodge, this self-registration campsite has a few hydro and water serviced recreation vehicle sites, tenting sites and showers.

Bed and Breakfasts: B&B facilities are springing up in the valley and surrounding area. Swan Road B&B near Kispiox Village on Swan Road and Poplar Park B&B run by Dave and Kathy Larson on Poplar Park Road are in the Valley and cater to fishermen and tourists. Wilfred Lee runs a B&B, but it is filled with his guided guests during steelhead season.

Recreational Service Campsites: There is a number of Forest Service camp sites in the valley. Most of these sites have a picnic table or two, an outhouse and a few campsites. The Upper Kispiox River Recreation site is located 26 miles from Hazelton on the upper Kispiox River. Sweetin River Recreation site, located at the junction of that river with the Kispiox, is another 20 miles upriver.

Guide Services

Three guides have steelhead days on this river: Wilfred Lee,

Jim Allen and Todd Stockner. All are long-time residents of the valley and know the river intimately.

Hook & Line Guiding: Wilfred Lee, the grandson of the Jack Lee who homesteaded in the valley in 1910, has lived in the Kispiox Valley all his 60 years. His father was the well-known big-game guide Jack Lee. Wilfred worked with his father for a number of years and guided his first clients for steelhead in 1958. In those early days, many of their sports were spin fishermen but he guided his first fly-fishers in 1959. Lee believes that in sport, method is everything and that's why he guides fly-fishers only. He gave up big-game guiding when the sports started using high-powered and scoped rifles capable of shooting an animal from 1000 yards. Not Wilfred's idea of sport.

He worked for Gord Wadley before purchasing Bob Clay's guide days in 1992 and since then has opened his B&B, which caters to his guide guests during fishing season. As a back fall for those days when the Kispiox is a raging torrent, he has days on the Bulkley, Skeena and Nass system.

Wilfred's clients come for chinook salmon in July and then from about the third week in August, he guides steelhead

Sweetin River Forest recreation site has limited camping.

through into November, when it gets too uncomfortable to fish due to the cold.

Guides always have some interesting tales about good catches as well as some interesting bigfish stories. The year 1998 was a super year on the Skeena system, the fish arrived early and in plentiful numbers. Lee remembers September 5,

1998, very well. A couple of clients were into 21 steelhead, the largest landed was a 42-inch male. An amazing day of fly-fishing.

Most of Lee's clients are from the USA, but others come from all over the world to fly-fish for the famous Kispiox steelhead. In recent years, he has had guests from Argentina, Sweden, Luxembourg, Italy, Spain, Tasmania and elsewhere. Many have never fished for steelhead. In the 2001 season, Wilfred's son Tom guided a first-time steelheader from Luxembourg. During the day, the sport landed two or three fish with a 42-incher the largest landed. However, in one of the last pools to fish Tom spotted three steelhead lying next to what he thought was a log. But the log moved and they realized it was a huge steelhead. Tom checked the gear making sure all was in order, especially the stout 25-pound-test-leader. Just in case this monster took, he didn't want the fish to break the sport's leader. The monster did take and during the fight the fish did break the 25-pound leader. Tom who has fished the river for years and has seen his share of big steelhead and chinook estimates the lost monster to be about 45 pounds.

Hook & Line Guiding (Wilfred Lee) phone: 250.842.5337

Kispiox Fishing Company: Run by Jim Allen, a fourth-generation Kispiox valley resident, Jim worked for Gord Wadley and bought Wadley's guide days in 2003. Like his cousin Wilfred Lee, Jim grew up on the banks of the Kispiox and has fished this river since boyhood. Jim's great grandparents were very early settlers in the area and it was on the water around his grandparent's Telegraph Trail Ranch, that Jim learned his steelheading skills. He and Wilfred have about the same number of days and like Lee, Allen's clients came from around the world to fly-fish for Kispiox steelhead. You can get in contact with Jim by phone or by email at: Kispiox Fishing Company, Jim Allen, 250.842.4055, or kispioxfishingco@hotmail.com.

Todd Stockner: Stockner has only 40 rod days for the

Gene Allen (left) and son Jim with a Kispiox steelhead

BRENT TAYLOR

Kispiox, compared to Allen's 193 days and Lee's 160 days. He lives in the valley and can be contacted at 250.842.6401.

The Future

We live in a resource-hungry world and who knows what demands will be put on the Kispiox, its valley and resources by future generations. The Kispiox valley is a flashy valley and subject to intense rains. The logging that took place in the last few decades of the 20th Century was typical of British Columbia forest practices of the day. They clear-cut to the river bank and ruined fish and wildlife habitat. Forest practices have improved, but we now have an environmentally insensitive government in Victoria. If the past is any indication of the future, then all crown-owned forest land and the streams that run through those lands that harbour fish will suffer. British Columbia is a have-not province in the Canadian Confederation. That has come about because for many decades, we have relied on resource extraction, whether it be forest or fish, that is non-sustainable. Because of those non-sustainable policies, politicians of all stripes over the decades have squandered the province's prosperity.

Valley residents have been pushing to protect the Upper Kispiox watershed since 1972. Concerned about headwater logging, the Valley's people came together, forming the Kispiox Watershed Coalition. Through their actions, they succeeded in getting park status for an area called Swan Lake Kispiox River Park in the river's headlands. In 2002, the Coalition managed to convince the powers-that-be to expand the upper Kispiox River watershed area considerably. Bob Clay and Wilfred Lee both agree that Park status for that area helps stabilize an already flashy system. However, local groups that value the fishery will need to maintain a vigilant watch against despoilers.

But other threats lurk out there that can cause harm to the famous stocks of steelhead. During the steelhead's migration along the coast, into the Skeena's huge estuary, and in the lower reaches of the Skeena River, the steelhead falls prey to commercial fishermen's nets. Throughout the Pacific Northwest, commercial interception of non-targeted stocks is a serious problem for weak stocks migrating with stronger ones. In fact, many Pacific Northwest stocks of coho, chinooks, and steelhead are facing extinction because of the century-long mixed-stock fishery strategy. Furthermore, enhancement activities such as the Fulton River and Pinkut Creek sockeye projects increased sockeye production in the Skeena system but to the detriment of the steelhead and other less numerous stocks. This is a complex problem with many stakeholders. Some progress has been made to better share the catch, but until the commercial fishermen adopt selective terminal inland fisheries, then steelhead and other lesser stocks of salmon will be threatened.

Sport fishers have been part of the problem and remain so. For years, too liberal sport limits had adverse effects on Kispiox steelhead stocks as well as those homing on other Skeena River tributaries. Catch-and-release since 1989 has helped rebuild depleted stocks. Skeena and tributaries sport fishers have plenty of opportunities to kill sockeye, pinks, chinook and in places coho as well as other game fish. The rebuilding of steelhead stocks has been a long, ongoing

Flat marshy lands with shallow lakes in the upper watershed are favourite places for viewing the valley's wildlife.

struggle with sacrifices made by Native, commercial, and sport fishers alike. Summer steelhead are special creatures with a released fish providing many times more value to the local economy than a dead commercial, Native or sport-caught steelhead. Unlike our forefathers who viewed the animals and fish as creatures there solely for man's exploitation, our role now is one of stewardship. We are the only creature on this earth that has the option to give life over death. Catch and release of steelhead by commercial, Native and sport fishers is the only long-term viable solution for a fragile species that will continually be affected by man's encroachment on its environment.

◆

During the drift, the raft glided through run after run. I had to pass by so much nice water if I wanted to get back to my truck and camper before dark. Jim Adams, Roger Still and John Bates too were drifting this section of river in their Watermasters. I too drifted alone and through the next mile or so of river we leap frogged from run to run.

Jim and I had passed Olga Walker's old camp a few runs back and I pulled into the left bank and Jim, the right. Roger and John joined Jim for a late lunch break. Just after I started to fish, Jim hollered across, "This is the run from which Mausser took his world-record fish." Hearing things across running water can be difficult at times and I waved acknowledgment.

It was about 3:00 p.m. when I cast my fly and the size 12 Woolly Bear Bomber started its waking through the surface film, chugging across my side of the river. I worked my way slowly down the run: cast, fish the fly, walk two paces, cast, fish the fly, walk two paces. Even on dull days, the September light can be quite bright and not the best light conditions to fish a waked fly. Because of the light conditions, I had on a smaller black Bomber. With Polaroid sunglasses in the mid-afternoon light I could see the river's structure better and some good stuff was coming up as I worked my way downriver.

My favourite double-hander fly rod—a 12-foot Bruce & Walker that I purchased in 1984—sent the Air Flo steelhead taper line out well. Angler, rod and line were performing so well that it prompted inquiries from Adams and gang across the river. Cast after cast went untouched, but then I sent the fly across the water and on this drift it would be coming across some large rocks. The thought had just passed through my mind that if I was going to get a fish, this is the spot. No sooner had that thought passed when the fly disappeared from the surface in a showy rise. With my audience watching, I played the fish bringing it to shore. I don't like to drag steelhead onto dry land and will play it out. When ready, I slide the fish into shallow water and when it goes onto its side I will stoop down and take the fly out. I followed that routine with this fish but when I started to put my rod down so that

This guy rose to a waked Woolly Bear Bomber in the run where Karl Mausser took his world record.

I could take the fly from the fish's mouth, it decided it wasn't quite happy to be where it was and scooted back into the river. The second time I brought the fish to shore it lay idle. I slid the hook from its mouth, and holding it by the tail's wrist, I turned it towards the deep water and watched as it retreated into the depths and safety.

Karl's world record tipped the scales at 33 pounds. My male steelhead too had more than just the sex in common with Mausser's, mine too had 33 in its statistics. The 33, however, was its length and not its weight. Nonetheless, I took my bows as the audience across the river clapped. I left the run thinking what a river and what a fish. The Kispiox River and its steelhead are a jewel. With sound management, anglers will be journeying to the River of Dreams in pursuit of this superb game fish for generations to come.